To Florence—
with love!

DAVE
THE
BOXER

by Evelyn Rothstein

Illustrated by Elizabeth Uhlig

MARBLE HOUSE EDITIONS

Published by Marble House Editions
96-09 66th Avenue (Suite 1D)
Rego Park, NY 11374
www.marble-house-editions.com

Library of Congress Cataloguing-in-Publication Data
Rothstein, Evelyn
Dave the Boxer/by Evelyn Rothstein

Summary: a young man growing up on the Lower East Side at the turn of the 20th century strives to be an amateur boxer in hopes of helping to support his family.

ISBN 0-9786745-8-8
Library of Congress Catalog Card Number 2007938951

Printed in China

To children everywhere who have to work before their time.

A long time ago in America, children from poor families often helped at home by going out to work instead of going to school. This is the story of Dave, who was one of those children.

Dave lived with his mother, sisters, and brothers on New York City's Lower East Side. Although he loved learning, Dave didn't go to school from the time he was seven years old until the time he was 12. Instead, he worked at different jobs.

His first job was as a delivery boy for a florist. Most of the time, Dave delivered flowers to funeral homes in his neighborhood. For this, the owner of the flower shop would pay him a dollar a week. Sometimes Dave also got tips. At the end of the week, Dave gave the money to his mother to help her pay for rent, food, and clothing for the family.

When Dave was nine years old, he saw a sign in the window of a tailor shop:

> Boy wanted to sweep and pick up pins.
> Also deliver clothes.
> Salary: $1.50 a week, plus tips.

I can do that, Dave thought. *And it will be good to get 50 cents a week more. Maybe I would get better tips too.* He went into the shop to ask about working there.

When the tailor met Dave, he liked him and gave him the job. And so for two years Dave swept the floor of the shop and delivered clothes to people in his neighborhood. Sometimes he made as much as three dollars for the week! Of course, he always gave the money to his mother.

When Dave was 11, he was out making a delivery one day and was spotted by a man driving a horse and wagon.

"How about helping me deliver coal to the houses in the neighborhood?" the driver asked Dave. "I'll pay you $3.00 a week and you'll probably get some good tips too."

Three dollars a week! thought Dave. *I would be able to give my mother more money.*

So Dave left his job at the tailor and started delivering coal. He was good at his job and worked very fast. Sometimes at the end of the week he was able to give his mother as much as $4.00!

But somehow, even though Dave and his whole family worked, there never seemed to be enough money for rent, food and clothing.....

When Dave was 12 years old, his mother said, "Dave, you **must** go back to school. You may only work on the coal wagon a few hours in the afternoon."

Dave wanted to go to school, but he was worried about his mother. *How can I make more money to help her?* he wondered.

He looked around at the different jobs in his neighborhood. Some people had pushcarts and sold hot dogs and pickles. *That's hard work,* thought Dave. *I don't mind working hard, but I don't think that I could make enough money to help my mother by having a pushcart.*

He saw other people selling flowers on the street. "Five cents a bunch!" the sellers would call. But only a few people would stop to buy flowers, and when the weather was cold and rainy, there was no way to make any money. *I don't think that selling flowers would help my mother enough,* Dave decided.

Lots of boys were on the street selling newspapers. "Two cents for a paper, Mister!" they would call. The boys were out selling in rain, snow, and cold. *I would have to sell lots and lots of newspapers,* Dave realized, *and even then, I could hardly give my mother enough money.*

So Dave continued to work on the coal wagon in the afternoons and kept thinking, *What can I be that would help my mother have enough money?*

Then when Dave was 14, he began to visit a place called a Settlement House, where boys and girls could play ping pong or checkers or do sports. One of the sports was boxing. Dave liked to watch boxing and began to wonder. *Maybe I could be a boxer. I like boxing and I think boxers make more money than newspaper boys or flower sellers or even more than I do working on a coal wagon.*

Dave especially liked to watch a boxer named Benny Leonard. Benny had been boxing for two years and was on his way to becoming a champion. He had already won boxing matches against all the boys in the Settlement House and would soon be ready to challenge a real winner. Dave had heard that boxers even make some money when they lose and get lots of **good** money when they win. *I will try to be like Benny Leonard*, Dave thought.

So whenever Dave wasn't in school or working on the coal wagon, he went to the Settlement House. He would watch the way Benny moved and punched and used his feet. He would practice doing whatever Benny did. Soon he got to know Benny and Benny would give him some tips about boxing.

"You have to be light on your feet. Keep balanced and always keep your hands up to protect yourself. Don't become an easy target. Just hit fast and hard."

After a few months of practicing what Benny showed him, Dave hoped to find someone to box with so that he could get real experience. *I'm getting good at this*, he thought. And he was!

Dave was soon beating all the boys in the Settlement House. *I think I'll make it as a boxer. Maybe I'll even get as good as Benny. Then I'll make enough money to really help my mother.*

Then one unbelievable day, Benny came over to Dave with his boxing manager.

"I think Dave is ready for a real match," Benny said to the manager. "I've been watching him move and punch. He has a great right hand, and he's always practicing."

Dave was overwhelmed with joy. Benny Leonard, the great Benny Leonard, had been watching *him* and now was talking about *him* to the manager!

"Well, if Benny thinks you're good, that's good enough for me," said the manager. "I'll set you up next week with one of our new champs and if you can keep up with him, well then, who knows?"

"I can do it," Dave promised. "I'll practice every day and watch how Benny does it."

Dave was at the Settlement House before school, at six o'clock in the morning. And then he'd come back at seven in the evening, after school and working on the coal wagon. He jumped rope, hit the punching bag, and watched every movement that Benny made.

Dave used some of the money from his job to buy new boxing gloves, boxing shorts, and the right shoes.

"I think you'll make it Dave," Benny would say. "I think you have what it takes to be a boxer."

A few weeks later, the manager spoke to Dave. "I think you're ready for your first amateur boxing match. It will be in the gym of the Settlement House and there will be five amateur matches. Each winner will then have a chance to try out for a professional match."

Dave was overjoyed. "There's big money in a professional match," he told his mother. "If I can get to be in professional matches, we'll be on Easy Street."

On the night of the match, the manager gave Dave a special "good luck" gift. "Here's your boxing robe," the manager said, handing him what seemed like a magical cloak.

Dave was thrilled and excited. He was hoping to win. "I always give a new boxer his first robe," the manager continued. "Oh, and one other thing, Dave," he added. "I'm giving you a new name. Dave Bierman doesn't sound like the name of a boxer. I'm announcing you tonight as Terry Hudson, a name people will remember."

And so Dave, now Terry Hudson, prepared to go into the ring. At that moment, he saw his opponent for the first time. *He's bigger and heavier than I am*, Dave worried. *I think he's done this before, too. What if I can't do it? What if he knocks me out with the first punch?* Dave was a bit scared, but he couldn't give up now.

"Good luck, Dave!" Benny shouted from a ringside seat. "You can do it!"

Dave took his seat in the corner of the ring, opposite his opponent. His manager stood next to him. "I think you can do it, Terry. You can do it," he assured him.

A man called a *referee* then walked into the center of the ring and announced the match. "Ladies and gentlemen," he said, "tonight you are about to see two great boxers. But only one of them will win. First is Max Kelly, weighing in at 135 pounds with a record of 15-2, with seven knockouts. Challenging Max, at 125 pounds and for the first time in the ring, is an exciting new boxer, Terry Hudson."

Dave looked at his opponent, Max Kelly, and worried again. *He's more than 135 pounds. I'll just have to stay on my feet and keep out of his way till he gets tired.* But Dave had no more time to think. The bell rang and he was on his feet into the ring.

The crowd was already cheering. "Go, Max!" they shouted. "Knock that skinny guy out! You know how to do it!"

Only Benny was shouting, "You can do it, Dave! Give him your right!"

For a couple of minutes, Dave kept Max from hitting him. He moved nimbly around the ring, dodging Max's punches. Max pushed Dave against the ropes, but Dave managed to slip out and keep moving. The bell would ring soon and Dave knew that if he didn't get hit, the first round would be over and he could go on.

Max was getting angry. No skinny amateur was going to beat him! His fists were ready to strike when the bell rang. The referee motioned for the fighters to go back to their corners.

"You're gonna have to start hitting, Terry," the manager warned, "or the fans are gonna boo you out. You can't be a boxer by just jumping around the ring."

The bell rang for the second match. Max and Dave came toward one another, each with his hands ready to do a knockout punch. Dave hit first, but missed. Everyone booed. He hit again, this time getting Max in the stomach. Everyone cheered. Dave was about to hit again, but Max moved too fast.

Dave could see that Max was moving faster than he had ever seen a fighter move! He lifted his right arm to punch and missed again. It was too late. Max swung a right into Dave's stomach. Dave was just catching his breath when Max hit again. One hundred thirty-five pounds against one hundred twenty-five pounds.

Dave fell against the ring and slipped down to the floor. He heard the referee count, "One, two, three, four, five, six, seven, eight, nine, ten...." He couldn't get up, but he could hear the referee's words, "The next professional champion of the boxing world...Max Kelly!"

Benny came into the ring and helped Dave up. "You made it to the second round, Dave. Not bad for a guy just starting out. You'll just get back into shape...."

But Dave knew that he wasn't a boxer. "No, Benny," he said. "I don't think boxing is for me. I'm too skinny and too scared. I'm afraid to get hurt and I can't be in the ring just dancing around, keeping away from punches. I'll just have to learn to do something else."

Dave went home. He put away his gloves and his shorts and his shoes. Then he went down to the Settlement House and gave his boxing robe to a 14 year-old boy who was practicing at the punching bag. He said good bye to Benny. *I'll have to find another way to make money to help my mother.*

Later that evening, Dave walked from the Settlement House up a wide street called Second Avenue. All over Second Avenue there were new theaters called *vaudeville houses*. They had signs outside telling of new music shows and comedy acts. Someone named Eddie Cantor

was in a song and dance show. A few streets up, a singer named Sophie Tucker was opening in a new show. Two streets after that, in another vaudeville house, Dave saw a poster of an actress named Mae West. *I'll bet these people will be famous some day*, he thought to himself.

Dave continued to look at the names and the signs on the theaters. *These people must make **good** money*, he thought. *Actors and singers are popular and people will pay **good** money to see them.* Dave kept walking and thinking. *Maybe I could work in a theater. I could learn to sing and dance and tell jokes and stories. Maybe I could learn to do those things and make enough money to help my mother. Maybe....*

Dave walked back home, still talking in his head. *If I can't be a boxer, maybe I can be in vaudeville. I'll try to get a job backstage and watch what happens on the stage. I'll learn how to do what actors do.*

31

So Dave began to make plans about learning to sing and dance and tell jokes. He practiced every morning before he went to school and every evening after working on the coal wagon. Then one day....

...but that is another story.

Some of the people mentioned in this story actually lived and were famous when Dave was a boy. You can find their names on the Internet and learn more about them:

Benny Leonard
Eddie Cantor
Sophie Tucker
Mae West

You might also want to know more about these topics:

Boxing in America
Vaudeville Theaters
Settlement Houses
The Lower East Side

Finally, if you are studying about the time when many children had to work instead of going to school, you can go to the Internet and search: Child Labor Laws in America.